CONTENTS

Marta Vieira da Silva	Footballer	6-9
Rui Naiwei	Go Player	10-13
Karen Uhlenbeck	Mathematician	14-17
Wang Yaping	Astronaut	18-21
Jane Goodall	Zoologist	22-25
Carolyn Bertozzi	Physicist	26-29
Fan Jinshi	Archaeologist	30-33
Shirin Ebadi	Lawyer and judge	34-35
Zaha Hadid	Architect	34-35
Tu Youyou	Pharmacist	36
Emmeline Pankhurst	Political activist	36
Kiran Mazumdar-Shaw	Entrepreneur	37
Ingrid Daubechies	Physicist	37
Zhang Weili	Martial Artist	38
Josephine Reynolds	Firefighter	38
Jane Campion	Filmmaker	38
Fei-Fei Li	Computer scientist	39
Dilma Rousseff	Politician	39
Simone Young	Conductor	39
Cassandre Beaugrand	Triathlete	40
Margaret E. Knight	Inventor	40
Cecilie Skog	Explorer	40
Dorothy Levitt	Racing driver	40
Federica Mogherini	Diplomat	41
Wangarĩ Maathai	Environmentalist	41
Christine Lagarde	Lawyer	41
Dong Hongjuan	Mountaineer	41

Yu Rong is an internationally recognised, multi-award-winning picture book illustrator. She is a Guest Professor at Soochow University and Director of the International Communication Research Centre for Jiangnan Culture. Yu Rong's distinctive artistic style combines paper-cut art with pencil sketching, seamlessly integrating Western modelling techniques with traditional Eastern aesthetics. Yu Rong has won the prestigious BIB Golden Apple Award and has received awards and acclaim across the globe.

Yu Rong

Yu Yi is a picture book author, her work includes Thump! Thump! Thump!, A Ray of Light, The Cat that Has Visited a Million Cities, and Eiffel and His Tower. She has been recognised with a Special Mention in the Bologna Ragazzi Award and the Bing Xin Children's Literature Award. Yu Yi's work has been recommended by the Ministry of Education in China. Her copyrights have been exported to the UK, Italy, Australia, New Zealand, South Korea, Croatia, Vietnam, Arab countries and other regions.

Yu Yi

Illustrators and figures illustrated:

Yu Rong — Illustration supervision and backgrounds
Li Qiongzhou — Marta Vieira da Silva
Hannah Rogerson — Rui Naiwei
Hannah Forrester — Karen Uhlenbeck
Li Qiongzhou — Carolyn Bertozzi
Wu Yingying — Wang Yaping
Wu Yingying — Jane Goodall
Maria Stuart — Fan Jinshi

Jake Hope

Jake Hope is the Awards Executive for the Carnegie Medals, the UK's oldest and most prestigious children's book awards. He is an award-winning librarian and is Publisher Liaison for the charity, Inclusive Books for Children. Jake has written books on reading development and visual literacy as well as picture books for children, including *Ming the Panda* which he collaborated on with Yu Rong.

Wu Yingying — Wu Yingying teaches at the Department of Fine Arts at Soochow University. Her research focuses on illustration and creativity. Wu Yingying has won numerous awards and her work has been exhibited widely.

Hannah Rogerson — Hannah Rogerson is an illustrator based in the North of England. Hannah has a passion for female led stories and is a firm believer in creating and promoting uplifting, untold female-led stories.

Li Qiongzhou — Li Qiongzhou is a faculty member in the Department of Textile and Fashion Design at the School of Art, Soochow University, China, and a visiting scholar at De Montfort University in the UK. Li Qiongzhou enjoys creating illustrations and comics in her spare time.

Hannah Forrester — Hannah Forrester is an illustrator from North Wales. She enjoys bright colours, creating children's books and making comics. Hannah found it fascinating researching the inspirational women included in this book.

Maria Stuart — Maria Stuart is an educator and picture maker. Maria grew up in the UK and throughout her life has been drawing and telling stories through the pictures she creates. Maria's teaching and illustration practice is built on her curiosity for the world.

WE is a Fox & Ink Books book

First published in Great Britain in 2026 by
Fox & Ink Books
University of Lancashire
Preston, PR1 2HE, UK

Co-published by 21st Century Publishing Group and Jiangxi Fine Arts Publishing House

Text copyright © Yu Yi, 2026
Illustrations © The Yu Rong Creative Team, 2026

978-1-916747-87-6

1 3 5 7 9 10 8 6 4 2

The right of Yu Yi and The Yu Rong Creative Team to be identified as the author and illustrators of this work respectively has been asserted in accordance with the Copyright, Designs and Patents Act, 1988.

This series has been developed in partnership with the Centre for the International Communication of Jiangnan Culture at Soochow University.

All rights reserved. No part of this publication may be reproduced, stored in a retrieval system, or transmitted in any form or by any means, electronic, mechanical, photocopying, recording or otherwise; or be used to train any AI technologies without the prior permission of the publishers. Fox & Ink Books expressly reserves this work from the text and data mining exception subject to EU law.

Translated by Jake Hope.
Designed by Yu Rong.

A CIP catalogue record for this book is available from the British Library. Printed and bound in Great Britain by Page Bros. UK.

Pioneering women from around the world

Written by YU YI   Designed by YU RONG
Translated by JAKE HOPE

Fox & Ink Books

This world-famous footballer grew up in a Brazilian town called Dois Riachos, meaning *two little rivers*.

The youngest of four children, she played football barefoot in the dusty streets.

Dreaming of being a footballer, her favourite player was Rivaldo. As a role model, he was second only to her mum, who was a single parent and always defended her daughter's right to play.

Her first pair of football boots was given to her by the grandfather of one of her teammates. She stuffed them with newspaper because they were too big.
She became the top scorer for the school's football team.

When she was a teenager, she saved enough money to take a bus ride for three days to travel to Rio for a trial with the Vasco da Gama club. What happened next was groundbreaking . . .

This footballer has played in the World Cup five times, scoring seventeen goals and becoming the top-scoring player in World Cup history. She has been honoured as FIFA's *Player of the Year* six times and has been described as the biggest name in women's football.

Her name is Marta Vieira da Silva. She is commonly known just as Marta.

'Fight to prove everyone wrong — everyone who thinks there is no place for girls on the pitch. Fight against their prejudice.'

Go is a game of tactic and skill dating back thousands of years. This world champion Go player was born in Shanghai in China. As a child, she wore glasses and was quiet and shy, but loved doing calligraphy!

When she began playing Go she found she enjoyed the feeling that came when she won. This motivated her to try to win more often!

As a teenager, she joined the Shanghai city Go team and found she loved thinking, planning and deciding how to play. Her confidence grew and she joined the national team.

She became the first professional Go player to achieve 9-dan ranking, a system of measuring a player's ability.

At twenty-nine she made it to the semi-finals of the 'Go Olympics' Ing Cup and was the last player to study under Go Master Wu Qingyuan.

What happened next was groundbreaking . . .

This Go player has defeated some of the greatest male Go players in modern history including the 'Stone Buddha' Lee Changho and 'Go Emperor' Cho Hunhyun. She won the National Go Championship and has secured the world championship title eight times.

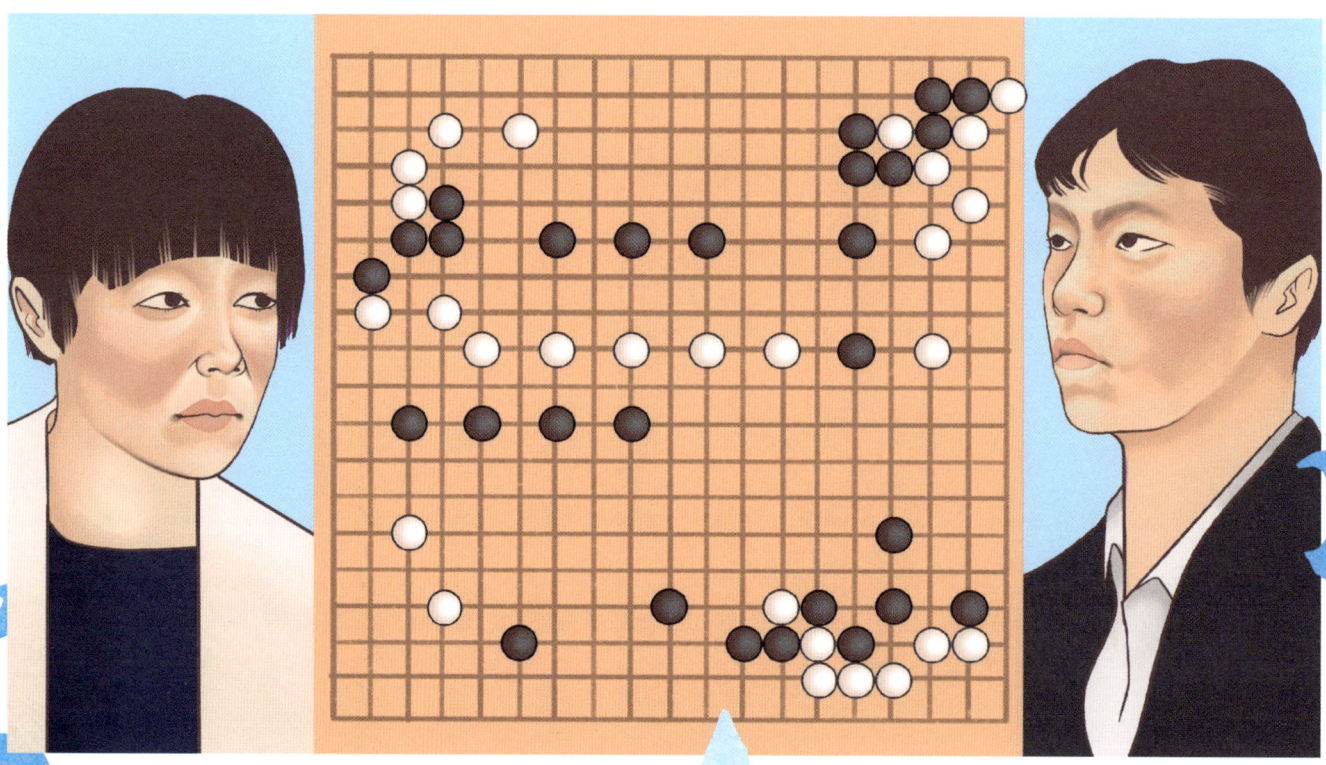

Her name is Rui Naiwei.

'If I didn't play Go, I would definitely not be who I am now. That timid and shy girl slowly grew into who I am today with the training and guidance of Go.'

This mathematician was one of the founders of geometric analysis and was born in Ohio, USA. Her mother was an artist and her father was an engineer. She grew up in the countryside where she loved playing football.

Another passion was reading about science. She was fascinated by the patterns of logic she read about.

After school, she was admitted to the University of Michigan's physics department where she discovered a love for what she called 'the structure, elegance and beauty of mathematics.' After graduating, she eventually went on to study for a doctorate in Mathematics, but when it came to looking for jobs, she was told people didn't hire women. She didn't stop trying and was eventually hired by the University of Illinois where she was promoted to Professor.

She co-founded the Women and Mathematics Programme at the Institute for Advanced Study to help offer women more chances in mathematics.

What happened next was groundbreaking...
In 2019 she became the first woman to win the Abel Prize, the highest award in mathematics.

Her name is **Karen Uhlenbeck**.

'We were told that we couldn't do math because we were women I liked doing what I wasn't supposed to do, it was a sort of legitimate rebellion.'

This record-breaking astronaut was born in Shandong, China.

As a child, after finishing her chores on the farm where she lived, she would gaze up at the stars from the cherry orchard.

She secretly applied to go to high school without her parents knowing. When she was seventeen, she entered the Changchun Flight Academy. She became a transport aircraft pilot flying four different kinds of fighter planes.

Seeing the brilliant tail flames of the Shenzhou 5 Rocket, she decided she wanted to be an astronaut! She took part in intensive interviews and spent a long time being trained in nearly a hundred subjects.

What happened next was groundbreaking . . .

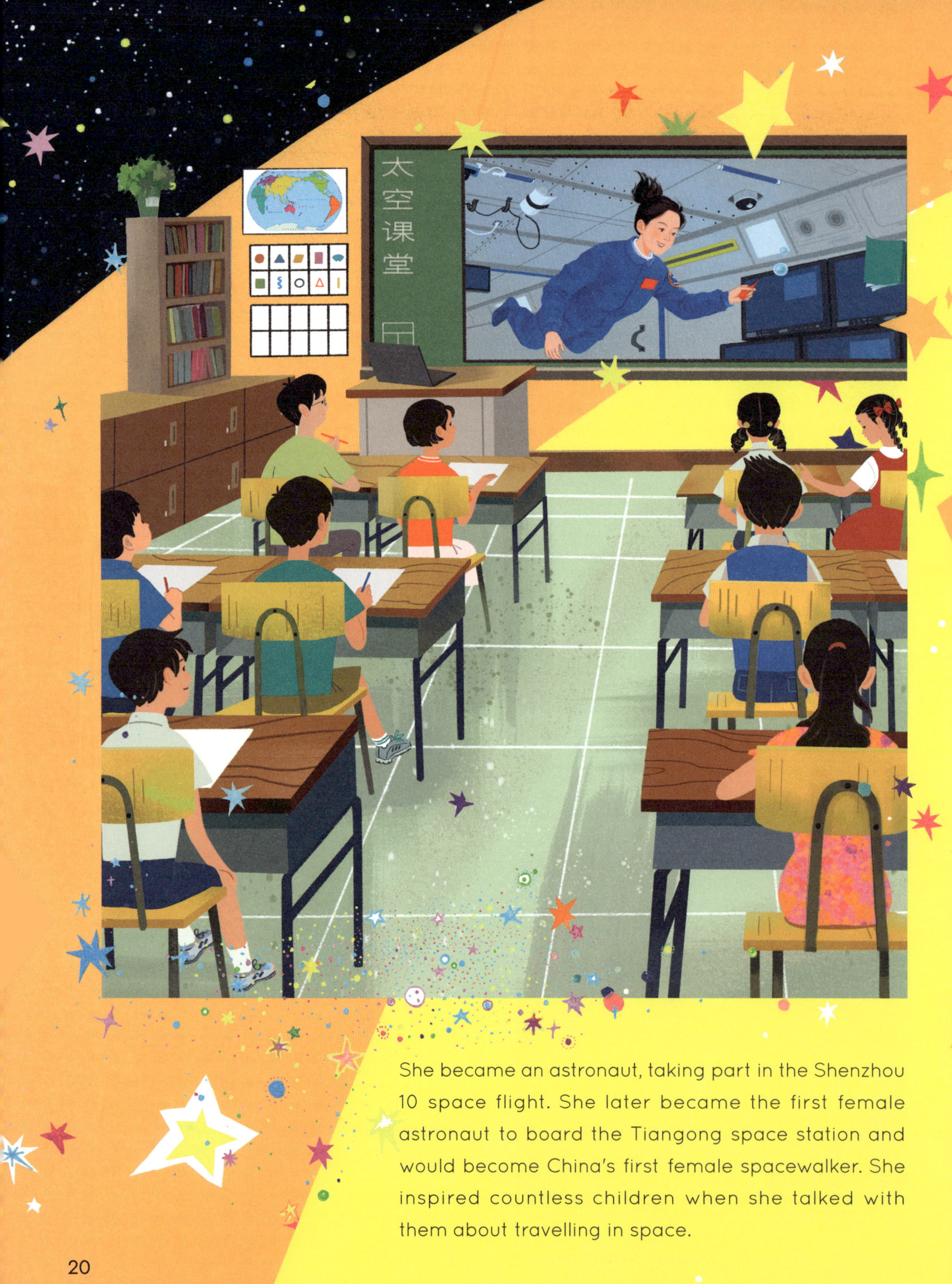

She became an astronaut, taking part in the Shenzhou 10 space flight. She later became the first female astronaut to board the Tiangong space station and would become China's first female spacewalker. She inspired countless children when she talked with them about travelling in space.

Her name is **Wang Yaping**.

'Dreams are like stars in the universe, seemingly out of reach, but as long as you work hard, you will be able to touch them one day.'

This zoologist is one of the world's leading experts on chimpanzees and was born in London, England.

Even at the age of four, this young girl was curious about the natural world. Wondering how hens laid eggs, she crept into the wooden henhouse at her grandmother's farm to see for herself.

She loved to watch creatures from the natural world and discovered lots through observing insects, birds and even earthworms.

As a child, she loved climbing the beech tree in her garden where she would read. She decided she wanted to go to Africa to discover more about wild animals.
In her early twenties she had saved enough money to buy a ticket to travel to Kenya. She walked alone into ancient jungles where nobody had dared to step foot.
What happened next was groundbreaking ...

In the jungle she walked freely among snakes and beasts and slept under the canopy of trees. Through her close observation of chimpanzees, she discovered that they use tools. Her favourite chimpanzee used blades of grass that he'd crafted to 'fish' for termites. Before this time, scientists believed humans were the only creatures capable of making tools.

Her name is Jane Goodall.

'When I look back over my life, it's almost as if there was a plan laid out for me – from the little girl who was so passionate about animals who longed to go to Africa and whose family couldn't afford to put her through college.'

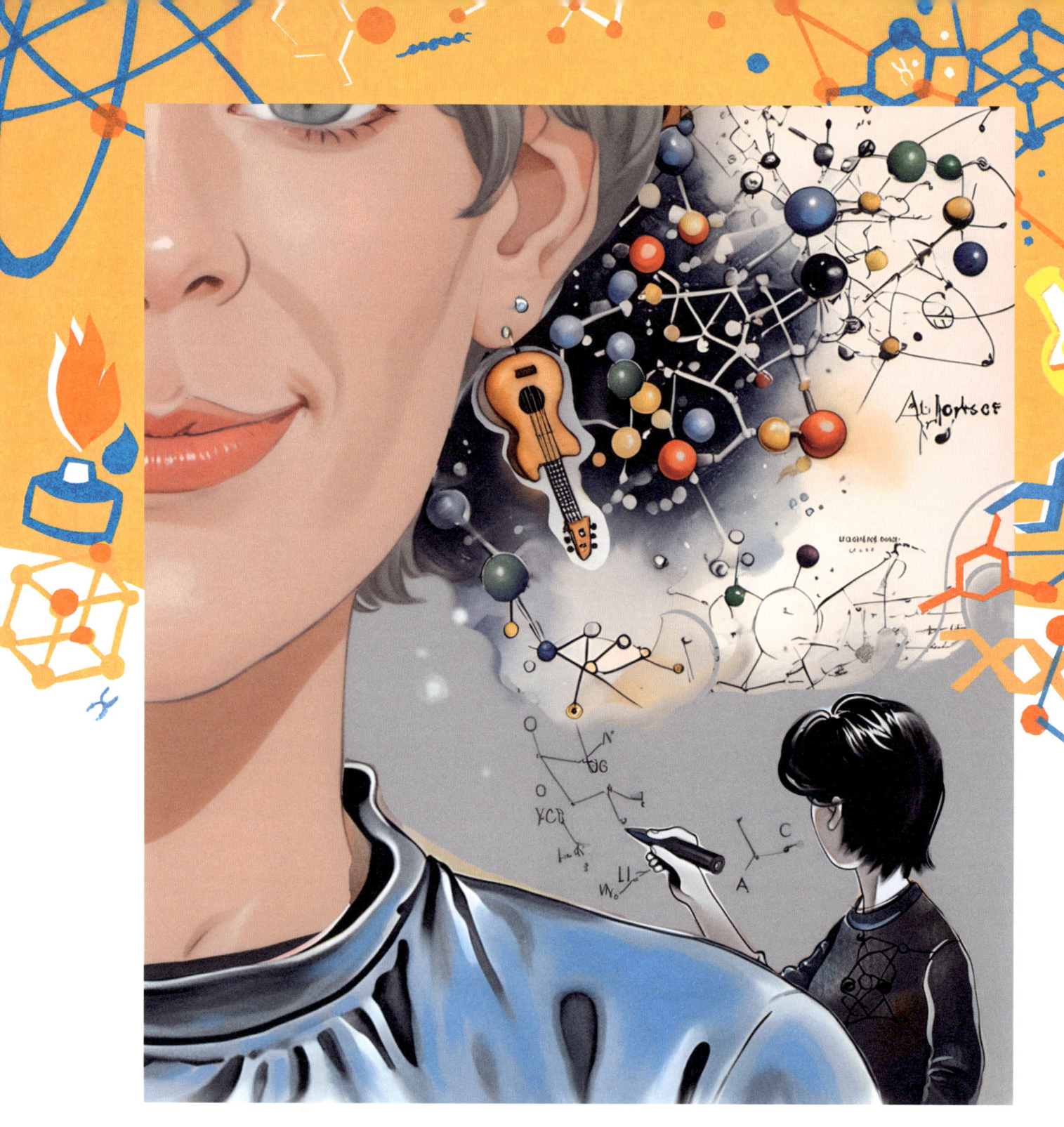

This Nobel prize-winning scientist was born in Boston, USA.
She was one of three sisters. Her father was a professor of nuclear physics and her mother was a secretary in the physics department. When her and her sisters were asked what they wanted to be, they all agreed on one job – a nuclear physicist!

A keen football player, she won her place at Harvard University because of her achievements in sports.

She formed a popular heavy metal rock band. Her interest in chemistry grew out of organic chemistry classes which many of her classmates found gruelling and difficult. She thought the classes were a good match for how her brain worked!

What happened next was groundbreaking . . .

She earned a PhD in Chemistry and took over a lab. Since then, she has won countless awards including the MacArthur Genius award.

Her name is Carolyn Bertozzi.

'It's easy to get spooked by a big challenge, but you're not supposed to do it in a day.'

This archaeologist is the honorary president of a research academy and was born in Beijing, China and grew up in Shanghai.

Early in her adulthood she battled sandstorms and pests to journey alone to the deserts to research and conserve a network of grottoes and Buddhist temples called the Mogao Caves. She spent many years living in adobe houses — homes made of dried mud bricks — and sleeping on clay beds, eating coarse grains.

She became the director of the Dunhuang Research Institute where she digitally archived every cave, mural and statue, helping to preserve thousands of years of fascinating history and culture.

She founded the Digital Dunhuang database, allowing the art and culture of Dunhuang's caves to be available across the whole world and has since written *The Complete Collection of Dunhuang Grottoes.*

Her name is Fan Jinshi.
People call her 'The Daughter of Dunhuang'.

'Compared with thousand-year-old caves, human life is very short. In our short lifetimes we should do our best to protect the past, helping others to learn from it.'

34

Her name is **Shirin Ebadi.** This lawyer and judge is from Hamadan, Iran. She fights for democracy and human rights. She was awarded the Nobel Peace Prize for her dedication to women's and children's rights.

Her name is **Zaha Hadid.** This architect was dubbed The *Queen of Curves.* Born in Iraq, she studied in England and Switzerland. Her work boldly uses space and geometric structures to break established practices in architecture. Zaha won the Pritzker Architecture Prize, one of the highest international awards for architects.

Her name is **Tu Youyou**. This Chinese pharmacist discovered artemisinin, a drug used to treat malaria which has saved millions of lives. She was awarded the Nobel Prize in Physiology or Medicine in 2015.

Her name is **Emmeline Pankhurst**. She was a political and social activist who helped organise the Suffragette movement in England. Her spirit for justice and equality helped to earn women the right to vote.

Her name is **Kiran Mazumdar-Shaw**. She is a technology entrepreneur from India. She started her company from scratch, forming Biocon, India's largest biotechnology company.

Her name is **Ingrid Daubechies**. She is a Belgian physicist and mathematician and the former president of the International Mathematical Union. Her work in wavelet theory and time-frequency analysis led her to become the first woman to win the Wolf Prize in Mathematics.

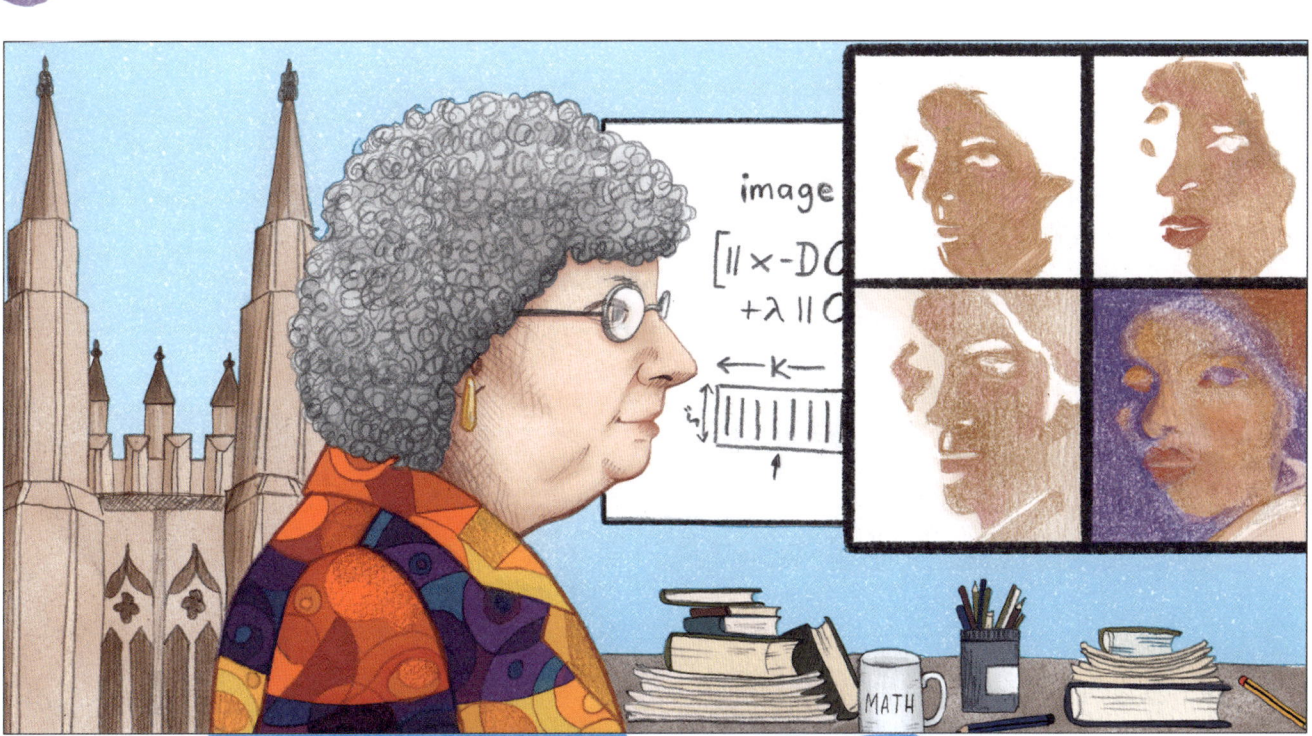

Her name is **Zhang Weili**. She is a mixed martial artist who defended her Ultimate Fighting Championship gold belt.

Her name is **Josephine Reynolds**. She was the UK's first woman to be a full-time firefighter.

Her name is **Jane Campion**. She is a multi-award-winning filmmaker. She was the first female director to win the sought-after Palme d'Or prize.

Her name is Fei-Fei Li. She is a computer scientist and inventor of ImageNet. Her work has aided the development of AI to support human progress.

Her name is Dilma Rousseff. She is a politician and was the first woman to hold the Brazilian presidency.

Her name is Simone Young. She is a conductor and winner of the Sir Bernard Heinze Memorial Award for outstanding contributions to music in Australia.

Cassandre Beaugrand, Olympic Gold-Medal-winning triathlete.

Margaret E. Knight, inventor who became a symbol for women's empowerment.

Cecilie Skog, adventurer and explorer who made the first unassisted trek across Antarctica.

Dorothy Levitt, first British female racing driver.

Federica Mogherini, politician and diplomat who served as Vice-President of the European Commission.

Wangarĩ Maathai, environmentalist and first African woman to win the Nobel Peace Prize.

Christine Lagarde, politician, lawyer and President of the European Central Bank.

Dong Hongjuan, mountaineer and first woman to conquer all of Earth's fourteen mountains that are over 8000 metres tall.

These are their stories. They have changed and shaped the world with their leadership, vision and determination. By pushing their minds, bodies and imaginations, they have broken barriers and opened doors for every one of us.

We can join with them so that all of us share a better future together as one, as **we**.

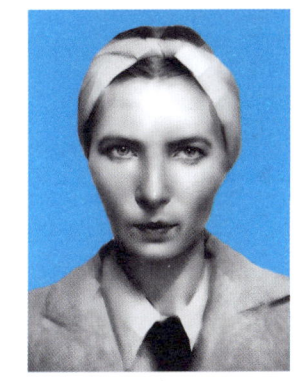

48

Qiu Jin — He Xiyu
Wen Weiqi — Li Wen Marie Curie
Beatrix Potter — Michèle Mouton — Zhang Xiyu
Zhang Guimei — Bian Yuchen
Yayoi Kusama — Yang Liping
Cleo Laine — Lin Xinhui
Frida Kahlo — Alison Brumwell
Ni Xialian — Wang Wenqi
Zhang Shuzhi — Chen Jiannan
Chen Yan — Wang Jiayi
Liu Hui — Wu Sijun
Shan Wen — Leng Nianze
Wu Yifang — Wu Sijun
Wang Zumin
Chun Lan
Zhu Xiaocheng

Zhou Mengyuan — Wu Yingying
Ruth Bader Ginsburg — Guo Cancan
Bei Mian — Xiang Jing Xu Fengcan — Li Limin
Ariana Grande — Bobby Holmes
Simone de Beauvoir — Zhong Huiyu
Liu Hulan — Zhou Xinyi Wan Jili — Huang Zhen
Sun Yingsha — Zhang Danyang
Karen Ghavri — Su Danni Guo Jinlan — Zhao Zhifeng
Maryam Mirzakhani — Lu Lifan
MalalaYousafzai — Denise K. Ainsworth
Eileen Chang — Bian Zening
Jane Austen — Lin Xinhui Niki de Saint Phalle — Wei Dongni
Wang Zhenyi — Zhang Jiangyue
Monther Teresa — Qiu Yuluo
Serena Williams — Zheng Xinyu
Zheng Qinwen — Fan Zixuan
Xu Jiaqiu R.A. Kartini — Sharleen Sutjitra
Hang Jifang Liu Yang — Xu Yinghong
Cao Aiqin — Yu Rong Lin Huiyin — Hu Jing
Amelia Crouch — Zheng Kaijia
Guo Jingjing — Jiang Yuhan
Audrey Hepburn — Yang Kang
Amelia Earhart — Wang Keyi
Käthe Kollwitz — Shen Ning
Huang Daoqo — Zhou Weiqi
Tan Chu

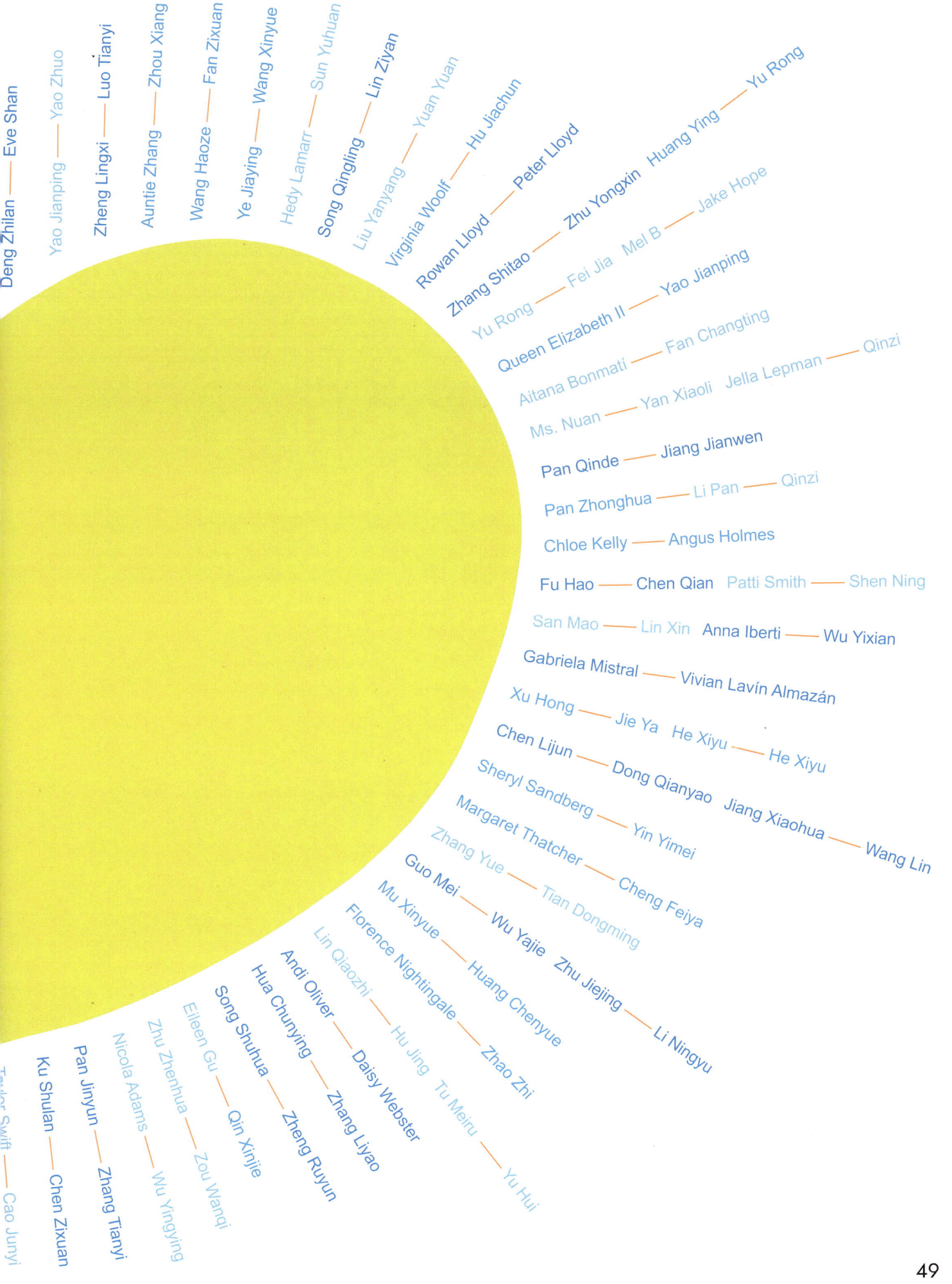

Illustrators and figures illustrated:

School of Art,
Soochow University
Tang Yucheng

Shirin Ebadi

School of Art,
Soochow University
Jin Yihan

Zaha Hadid

School of Art,
Soochow University
Wu Na

Tu Youyou

WE was created in an exciting and innovative way.
The stories of different pioneering women were used to
create opportunities for new artists to illustrate each character.
Staff and students from the School of Art at Soochow University and at the
School of Arts and Media, University of Lancashire, were given expert guidance
by multi-award-winning illustrator Yu Rong, director of the International
Communication Research Centre for Jiangnan Culture at Soochow University.

In addition to the students and staff who created illustrations which
enhance the text, the book concludes with a gallery of female portraits.
These were crafted by many talented individuals from
across the world and represent inspirational
women who have helped to shape
and influence their
creators' lives.

School of Art,
Soochow University
Lai Siqi

Emmeline Pankhurst

School of Art,
Soochow University
Guo Jiahang

Kiran Mazumdar-Shaw

School of Arts and Media,
University of Lancashire
Wendi Plaskett

Ingrid Daubechies

School of Art,
Soochow University
Chen Mu

Zhang Weili

School of Arts and Media,
University of Lancashire
Hannah Forrester

Josephine Reynolds

School of Art,
Soochow University
Shu Meng

Jane Campion

School of Art,
Soochow University
Zhang Wufeng

Fei-Fei Li

School of Art,
Soochow University
Wu Na

Simone Young

School of Arts and Media,
University of Lancashire
Maya Corry

Dilma Rousseff

School of Art,
Soochow University
Tang Yingyao

Cassandre Beaugrand

School of Art,
Soochow University
Wang Zhimeng

Margaret E. Knight

School of Arts and Media,
University of Lancashire
Hannah Hindle

Cecilie Skog

School of Art,
Soochow University
Wang Huiru

Dorothy Levitt

School of Art,
Soochow University
Wu Yingying

Wangarĩ Maathai

School of Art,
Soochow University
Li Wenxiao

Federica Mogherini

School of Art,
Soochow University
Cao Junyi

Christine Lagarde

School of Art,
Soochow University
Jiang Liyuan

Dong Hongjuan

Project supervisors

Yu Rong
Maria Stuart
Wu Yingying

GLOSSARY

AI
AI stands for artificial intelligence and is technology which helps computers to do tasks that would ordinarily require human thought. AI uses data and patterns to help solve problems.

ARCHAEOLOGIST
A historian who studies the past using buildings and artifacts that are often uncovered on digs.

BIOTECHNOLOGY
Using living things to help solve problems or to make useful products such as crops that are resistant to disease.

DEMOCRACY
A system of rule where everyone has a voice and is able to have a fair say.

ENTREPRENEUR
Someone who has good ideas for business and works hard and creatively to make these happen.

GEOMETRY
A branch of mathematics about the properties of points, lines and surfaces.

GO
An ancient board game for two players. It is played with black and white stones. Each player tries to fence off more space than the other.

MOGAO CAVES
A system of caves and temples located near Dunhuang in China.

NUCLEAR PHYSICIST
A scientist who studies atoms, some of the smallest particles of matter.

ORGANIC CHEMISTRY
The scientific study of substances containing carbon.

PHARMACIST
A person trained to prepare medicines to support people's health and wellbeing.

SUFFRAGETTES
Campaigners who fought for women to have the right to vote.

TIANGONG SPACE STATION
A permanently crewed, Chinese space station that orbits the Earth.

TIME FREQUENCY ANALYSIS
The study of how a signal's frequency can change over time.

TRIATHLETE
A sportsperson who competes in a race involving swimming, running and riding a bicycle.

WAVELET THEORY
A mathematical model for analysing signals and images by breaking them into small waves known as wavelets.

ZOOLOGIST
A scientist who studies how and where animals live.